Tickner's
HORSE&HOUND

Tickner's
HORSE&HOUND

J. A. Allen
London

British Library Cataloguing-in-Publication Data.
A catalogue record for this book is available from the British Library.

ISBN 0.85131.703.0

Published in Great Britain in 1997 by
J. A. Allen & Company Limited,
1 Lower Grosvenor Place, Buckingham Palace Road,
London, SW1W 0EL.

Typeset and designed by Judy Linard
Printed by Dah Hua Printing Press Co. Ltd., Hong Kong

Foreword

For some 20 years the late John Tickner's beautifully crafted cartoons appeared each week in *Horse & Hound*. They were guaranteed to raise a smile, sometimes guffaws of laughter, and they always made their point and hit home. Often they were drawn to illustrate a news item that had amused John, or something he had spotted on the Letters to the Editor page, sometimes just to draw to our attention the more pompous aspects of the horse world.

Into each cartoon, however, went the experience of a lifetime's observation of country life and of the many characters who enjoy working with horses or just spectating. John didn't just sit on the sidelines sketching, he was a countryman who enjoyed country sports to the full, particularly anything associated with the horse.

It will come as no surprise to anyone to learn that John Tickner could actually ride a horse, though he told me he had never been able to ride as often as he would have liked. He talked fondly of hunting in Kent as a young man and this was the inspiration for many of his hilarious cartoons on the subject.

Amongst his armoury as a cartoonist were great powers of observation, a shrewd ability to weigh up a person's or a horse's character, and a sparkling sense of humour which never set out to hurt, merely to point out the folly of our ways in dealing with that most noble animal the horse.

So often it is the horse's unfailing patience and good sense which rescues us from ridiculous situations which should never have arisen. John always looked at it from the horse's point of view and couldn't resist poking gentle fun at those of us who sometimes get far too serious about ourselves and our equestrian endeavours.

This collection of drawings will give you a good insight into the art of John Tickner. It is humour that will not fade and in ten or 20 years time you will still appreciate the fun which John Tickner had watching us all struggle to deal with horses and hounds in, well, not quite the way we intended.

A writer himself, John was also a former editor of a farm and country magazine in Kent, as well as a cartoonist, which explains his extraordinary ability to keep to deadlines. Having spent his early years in Kent, John moved on to Dorset before finally settling in Hereford with his devoted wife, Barbara.

He saw action in Burma in World War II with the South African Rifles, but seldom talked about his distinguished war service. He drew upon his links with South Africa in *Leopards in the Cellar*, his memoirs, which were published six years ago.

Even when John went into hospital in later life for bouts of surgery he would supply us with cartoons to tide us over the weeks he was to be away and I am told he could often be found sketching away in his hospital bed.

Quietly spoken, John was a true gentleman and through his rare gift managed to enhance the lives of the 350,000 readers of *Horse & Hound* who each week paused to look at Tickner's cartoon.

John died peacefully in his sleep at the age of 84 on March 1, 1997, but not before completing his last cartoon for the pages of *Horse & Hound*. In all the years John worked for us he was the complete professional and one of life's great enhancers. It was a privilege to have worked with him and I am sure that he would be delighted to have this volume as a fitting memorial to his work.

Without a doubt, and with apologies to Whyte Melville, we at *Horse & Hound* have to freely confess that 'for the best of our fun we owed it to John Tickner's cartoons'. I hope you enjoy thumbing through the pages of this latest collection of John's drawings.

Arnold Garvey,
Editor, *Horse & Hound*

'Traditionally one should get in as many days as possible in the saddle before Christmas.'

'That reminds me – I haven't ordered a bird for Christmas!'

'Stealing the Christmas turkey is not the fun it used to be.'

'Hounds have no imagination; every year they just ask for some
good scent!'

'I told you it wasn't real!'

'Those driving people tackle some extraordinary obstacles.'

'That's all we need!'

Christmas Eve.

'Low-flying aircraft are a menace!'

'The horses never seem fit just after Christmas.'

'A happy Christmas to one and all.'

The Field may not be larger after Christmas but its much heavier to carry!'

'I said that after all those festivities I'd never be able to face a hunter again!'

'It's good to be active again after sitting about during the festivities.'

'My New Year resolution was to hunt all day but the horse
disagreed!'

'The New Year is exciting. One never knows what lies ahead!'

'Do you think horses make New Year resolutions?'

'Two resolutions and three fences broken already this year!'

'The trouble about Christmas holiday hunting is that all those
children get in the way!'

'After the festive season one can be a loose horse for hours;
they can't run!'

'Perfect hunting weather!'

'I think they're being blown away.'

'What a pity we didn't get this Christmas card type weather
earlier!'

'In about one hundred years time they'll make jolly Christmas
cards out of this sort of thing!'

'What do you mean, isn't it pretty?'

'We got them in time for the thaw.'

'The thrill of the chase again, Colonel!'

' It is so nice to get back to normal now that it's thawed.'

'The fox blew away in that direction!'

'No Madam, I am *not* pony-trekking!'

'We don't exchange horse-talk; her family is not in the database directory!'

'Who said, the ideal place for a retired couple today is the peaceful British countryside?'

'To qualify a point-to-pointer you must attract the master's attention!'

'That's called "downwardly mobile"!'

'The popularity of point-to-point races emphasises the national love of horses!'

'She was advised to take a crash course before point-to pointing!'

'Well, at least the horses are in peak condition this season!'

'The start of the point-to-point season – they're off again!'

'She reserves the horse for the summer shows.'

'We made the gig ourselves.'

'It's such a relief to get away from all that town traffic.'

'Who was it that said women look their smartest in riding kit?'

'I think that's what they call "rode rage".'

'It's my effort for road safety. It says "if you are close enough to read this, your vehicle is about to be kicked".'

'Remember road safety – always give hand signals.'

'No courtesy these days – the chap didn't even say "thank you"!'

'She won't wear a safety helmet; she'd rather preserve her beauty than her brains.'

'They say that travelling backwards is less stressful for horses.'

'Equestrian sports are so good for young people, the horse has a civilising influence.'

'That's the new girl: she's studying equine psychology.'

'He's solved the problem of a dressage salute when wearing a chin strap.'

'They always walk like that; they're dressage judges.'

'Mother says, "does your family show in thoroughbred or non-thoroughbred classes?"'

'As I see it, you are agricultural if you stay outside and non-agricultural if you come in!'

'When I grow up I'm going to be a well-sponsored, champion eventer.'

'It says, "keep to the bridle path".'

'We're just retracing very old bridle-paths.'

'She's so keen on eventing she brings her work home with her!'

'It's the conformation of the hound show *judges* that worries me.'

'Restrictive practices!'

'Its a lovely beach for the children to dig holes in.'

'I don't think that's what the B.H.S. meant by the "horse-and bed-and-breakfast" scheme dear!'

'The camp accommodation is particularly good this year.'

'Out!'

'She's very supportive and keeps up with her daughter!'

'All these horses are making it dangerous for dogs!'

'The eventing influence has certainly livened up our gymkhana classes.'

'It seems the eventing season has begun!'

'Its such fun to have show-jumping outdoors again!'

'She probably thinks she's the perfect roll model!'

'It seems to be deeper than usual.'

'He's an all-round horseman.'

'She's quite happy sitting holding the reins while I go for a drink.'

'It's the setting that counts!'

'She probably tells her friends abroad that the photos were
taken in the back garden!'

'His seat was only marginal and he's losing it.'

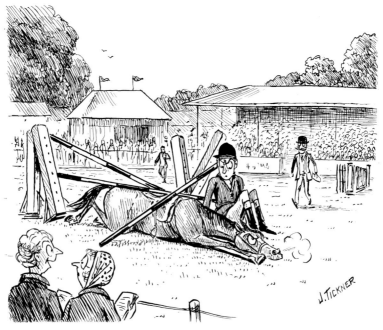

'They say he started as a Flat racehorse and now he's a flat show jumper.'

'In future, leave counting the strides to me.'

'He talks to horses, you know!'

'It's not a lap of honour – he's carrying a large part of the last fence.'

'I hear they're going to put hunting antiques into a special museum.'

'You got the name wrong again!'

'It's funny how his knees always bend when his height's measured.'

'Of course I had to send him off – he called me a moron!'

'This must be one of those non-working-hunter classes?'

'Her trouble is too much side and not enough saddle.'

'He said if he received one more complaint something would snap.'

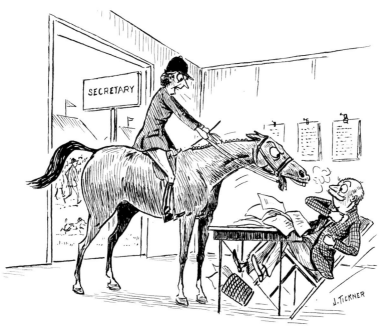

'Complaints Department?'

'They say he's purpose-bred but I can't imagine what the purpose was!'

'An egg-and-spoon and a bending race win and she thinks she's Horse-of-the-Year!'

'My daughter's pony is sure to carry off the cup this year.'

'She's all for collective equestrian activities.'

'They say some judges today seem to ignore bad-mannered show ponies.'

'My daughter's just judged the pony classes: I think they want her autograph.'

'He's good with children but he doesn't care for judges!'

'Now is *not* the time to remind me you were bred to be a show hack!'

Patience, humility, good manners: all things youngsters can
learn from their equine companions.

'Show-jumping would be more fun if someone set it to jolly music.'

'I believe he's competing in Calgary next month.'

'The shires are the ones with leg-warmers, dear.'

'Do we ask them to walk or float?'

'I've always said there's a place for the heavy horse on the land.'

'I think he hopes to be "the fox of the year"!'

'Sandy's been watching too much jumping on television.'

'He says the panniers are meant for grouse.'

'Remember conservation – don't frighten the birds!'

'*We* don't need a "rural charter" to help the economy of the countryside.'

'I told you we should have turned left!'

'It's only the referee.'

'Don't worry, we can go faster than this!'

'I repeat – you're off course!'

'Did you hear the suggestion that the banning of terriers might "modify" hunting?'

'I see they're still discussing the problem of overweight show hunters.'

'Cubhunting is the ideal opportunity to let children see what it's all about.'

'Romantic, these misty mornings, don't you think?'

'See anyone you know?'

'He's a staunch supporter of informal dress for cubhunting.'

'It's such fun to recognise the old cheerful faces at these early meets!'

'Well, they say a young horse should be kept away from hounds during cub hunting.'

'Father's been furious about the water shortage.'

'I can't understand why people like the trees to be bare when they start hunting.'

'The secretary's very hot on subscriptions.'

'The secretary is liable to drop on one unexpectedly.'

'It's not a lurking fox – it's a lurking secretary.'

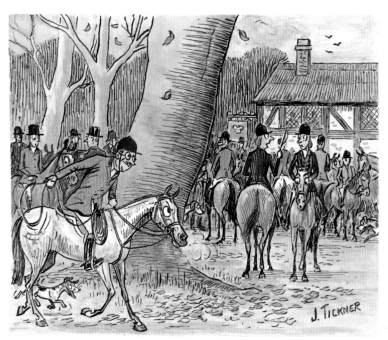

'They say the new secretary is a wild west enthusiast.'

'I asked if they were team-chasing and he said "no, just horse-chasing".'

'He was going to introduce his new horse to hounds but the terrier is introducing itself first!'

'The season may be starting but she's in no hurry.'

'That horse was advertised as "hunted on and off"! Mostly off I expect.'

'It's one of the new joint masters familiarising himself with the ground.'

'Our aerobics group would be proud of him.'

'I expect she's come to declare the meet open.'

'That must be what is called "drag- hunting"!'

'That horse usually follows a Harrier pack!'

'I did say take your fences as they come. I didn't say bring them
with you!'

'I hate all this violence brought by man to the countryside!'

'I see the colonel is going home early today!'

'That's his mother; her family has had agricultural status for generations.'

'That's funny, I always thought the horse jumped first.'

'Newcomers to fell hunting find the views breathtaking.'

'She said she'd make a splash if they had the meet at her place!'

'It was obvious that grey would be the fashionable horse colour
for 1998 but this is ridiculous!'

'He's new and I brought him along to show him hounds.'